"Keep eye contact with these poems. Susan Cowger pioneers the lamentable animal wilderness of suffering and reports back with language that coheres where there seemed only incoherence. Cowger conducts the passage through the ambivalence and confusion of pain with great care, such that, as we attend to these poems, we discover ourselves to be loved and tended well by both the poet and her Lord."
–MATTHEW CLARK, author of *Only the Lover Sings*

"A book of flight, dive, trill, and shriek, Susan Cowger's bold and riveting collection on cancer, *Hawk & Songbird*, takes away our breath and then infuses us with Spirit. These luminous poems brim with birds and tremble with omnipresent Coyote. Yet, in the midst of 'animal pain', the poet also howls love of family, friends, and the Divine. Even in 'darkness / darker than the darkness / of before', Cowger's necessary words rise and soar."
–MARJORIE MADDOX, author of *In the Museum of My Daughters Mind*

"Master word-crafter Susan Cowger gives her readers 'permission by example' for asking hard questions and living into them for answers bigger than words. It takes courage to ask and courage to receive the reply, but the asking and receiving is worth every moment of the conversation. As a seasoned and gracious sherpa, Cowger companions us into the greater unknowns faced by every mortal who hopes to live well and love deeply."
–LANCIA E. SMITH, publisher and executive director, Cultivating Oaks Press

"With equal parts transparency and generosity, Susan Cowger scatters her verses like birdseed to nourish the reader who marvels at the call and response of faith despite the roving shadow of predatory illness. This isn't just seed for the feeding, but also the planting, 'as God's promises run after us all / with a spade' to turn the hard soil of our hearts and help us see afresh that 'Being alive is a gate made of pearl.'"

–BRADFORD WINTERS, showrunner and poet

Hawk & Songbird

The Poiema Poetry Series

Poems are windows into worlds; windows into beauty, goodness, and truth; windows into understandings that won't twist themselves into tidy dogmatic statements; windows into experiences. We can do more than merely peer into such windows; with a little effort we can fling open the casements, and leap over the sills into the heart of these worlds. We are also led into familiar places of hurt, confusion, and disappointment, but we arrive in the poet's company. Poetry is a partnership between poet and reader, seeking together to gain something of value—to get at something important.

Ephesians 2:10 says, "We are God's workmanship..." *poiema* in Greek—the thing that has been made, the masterpiece, the poem. The Poiema Poetry Series presents the work of gifted poets who take Christian faith seriously, and demonstrate in whose image we have been made through their creativity and craftsmanship.

These poets are recent participants in the ancient tradition of David, Asaph, Isaiah, and John the Revelator. The thread can be followed through the centuries—through the diverse poetic visions of Dante, Bernard of Clairvaux, Donne, Herbert, Milton, Hopkins, Eliot, R. S. Thomas, and Denise Levertov—down to the poet whose work is in your hand. With the selection of this volume you are entering this enduring tradition, and as a reader contributing to it.

—D.S. Martin
Series Editor

Hawk & Songbird

Poems

SUSAN COWGER

CASCADE *Books* • Eugene, Oregon

HAWK & SONGBIRD
Poems

Copyright © 2024 Susan Cowger. All rights reserved. Except for brief quotations in critical publications or reviews, no part of this book may be reproduced in any manner without prior written permission from the publisher. Write: Permissions, Wipf and Stock Publishers, 199 W. 8th Ave., Suite 3, Eugene, OR 97401.

Cascade Books
An Imprint of Wipf and Stock Publishers
199 W. 8th Ave., Suite 3
Eugene, OR 97401

www.wipfandstock.com

PAPERBACK ISBN: 979-8-3852-1199-9
HARDCOVER ISBN: 979-8-3852-1200-2
EBOOK ISBN: 979-8-3852-1201-9

Cataloguing-in-Publication data:

Names: Cowger, Susan. | other names in same manner

Title: Hawk & Songbird : Poems / Susan Cowger.

Description: Eugene, OR: Cascade Books, 2024 | Series: Poiema Poetry Series.

Identifiers: ISBN 979-8-3852-1199-9 (paperback) | ISBN 979-8-3852-1200-2 (hardcover) | ISBN 979-8-3852-1201-9 (ebook)

Subjects: LCSH: subject | subject | subject | subject

Classification: call number 2024 (paperback) | call number (ebook)

02/12/24

To God
for the privilege of life

To Jesus
for daring to live as one of us

To my beloved Dana
for making this journey with me

To my traveling companions
for linking arms and for not being afraid

Loss has no presence. It reveals presence.

Contents

Preface | xi

To Save a Robin | 1

HOOKED BEAKS AND TALONS | 3

New Moon | 5
Before I Ask for Anything | 6
I Talk into My Hands | 7
Fast and Shallow | 8
Claws | 9
Float Across Azure | 11
Waiting for the Scan to Be Read | 12
Enough for Today | 13
Should You Cover That | 14
Speaking of Weather | 15
Momma   Was It Like This | 16
Poverty | 17
Holiest | 18
Burning with Ash | 19
Come Back   Coyote | 20
The Boy Sweeping Whispered   Love Fiercely | 21
Your Number's Up | 22

WINGS AND HOLLOW BONES | 23

Long Nights' Moon | 25
On The Observation Deck: A Resuscitation | 26
Canada Geese Sail | 27
When My Head Is Cold | 28
When I Pray to Be Healed | 29
All Ears | 30

Contents

Instruction in Case You Wake Early | 31
Sigh too Brief to Mention | 32
The Burden of Gifts | 34
The Wonder of Weeping | 35
Marriage | 36
Seventeen Houseplants | 38
Honey from a Rock | 39
Mud until Today | 40
Exaudi Nos Domini (Hear us Lord) | 41

A SONG IN THIS PLACE | 43

Blood Moon | 45
Momma What Did You Call | 46
The Conductor's Baton | 47
Summon This Kind of Prayer | 48
An Incident | 49
When a Rib Tears Away | 50
Wind Crying to Get In | 51
Putting on a Swimsuit | 52
She Says You Get What You Get | 53
Sugar Moon | 54
The Uncertainty Principle | 55
Too Close to My Eyes | 56
Memorial | 57
The Day Before We Leave Seattle | 58
Exposure | 59
My New Name | 60
A Valley Wide as Spring | 61
Escape | 62

A HAWK DOES NOT HAVE A SONG | 63

Sunrise and Moonset | 65
Immortal Invisible | 66
Coyote Alive | 67
Transfiguration | 68
Thirst of Shore Meets Parch of Water | 69
Behind the Blinds | 70
17 Degrees Snow Blinding Light | 71

Contents

Red-Tailed Hawk | 72
Symptoms of Morning | 74
Time Disappears (while painting) | 75
He of Old Age Died | 76
Dear Hawk | 77
Lunula | 78
Finding You Again | 79
Prayer Without Words | 80
Plumage   The Wing and Its Mighty Elbow | 81
Selah   To Understand More Than a Sentence | 82
The Precipice | 83
Care Giver | 84
What Happened | 86

AN AFTERWORD | 87

Breath Holding | 89

Acknowledgments | 91
Other Books in the Poiema Poetry Series | 93

Preface

Of sound mind and fine of feather, at the peak of pandemic panic, I was diagnosed with blood cancer: multiple myeloma. That season reminds me of a fledgling careening from the nest, now halfway to the ground.

So many questions . . . grabbing for hope and help.

These poems are not answers to questions. The words herein ponder the way life & death fly above us, circle us, heckle & intimidate, exhaust faith. This is about what we have—and what's left.

I call it a walkabout, the way one navigates treacherous unknowns with a solitary goal to keep moving and survive. You must look around.

A raptor lurks: death on a hunting spree. Cover your ears—a flurry of screeching calls will ensue. Any songbird's call-of-alarm is the universal language of terror—a higher frequency, closer to a scream. Myriads join the chase; assault the evil; get the killer.

It's called mobbing the hawk. Something like a prayer meeting . . .

I need these birds, these people.

Remember though, songbirds cannot harm a hawk, lead an injurious attack, or force a hawk to flee. But watch these small birds; take note how blackbird or kingbird, swift & agile, will dive-bomb, even ride a hawk. Claws dug in and perhaps wishing for talons, they selflessly protect their own. What causes such bravery?

I want courage like that.

Preface

You lionhearted songbirds—I'm still thinking about you grounded, feathers scuffing the dust, appearing wounded and unable to fly. With one daring performance songbirds hoodwink evil, draw away any who would kill their young, often to their own demise. Who sacrifices this way?

I want to be this kind of love.

I've watched red-tailed hawks for years. I call them Protectors, though I'm not sure I've ever seen a hawk chase my enemies; yet there they are the presence of power—think lightning speed, diving on prey at one-hundred-twenty miles per hour. Who embodies such audacious daring?

Lord God, be for me this dauntless protector.

To Save a Robin

A Husband Poem

> . . . *all my beloved can do is not enough*

We lock eyes   my wife and I   the clench
of her back spasm   barbaric   No
hitch or crick   one slight bend
holds breath hostage as
her face crumbles   I catch her hands

steady and cradle her down the steps
to the basement   to a safer harder bed
cooler air   peace & quiet   I've no words
for   *she cannot move*
Nothing to say or do   just wait it out

Ransacking prayers   I plead with God
check on her every other minute
My good ear against the door   a bump
a scare   panicked clawing screeches on glass
I burst in to find a baby bird in the window well

Benevolence falls to me   rescuing life
that flails at the softest touch   I hoist him out
on a shovel   nestle the bird near the end of the house

All the calls of distress   we the lost & found   bawl
for each other   It takes only two hours

and baby's back in the well   Salvation again falls

to me   Shoveling   shooing
the upset to the front garden   finding shelter
as God's promises run after us all
with a spade

And me covering the well
with a tarp   leaving my wife in darkness
darker than the darkness of before

Now here by her bed   I keep watch

Hooked Beaks and Talons

New Moon

Nary a crescent of light tonight

Where above the world are you   new moon
no moon   Waiting are you waiting
to make a move   or hiding   look who's hiding
a wince when the doctor's matter-of-fact tone
pronounces cancer   in the gibbous phase

Trusted light before dawn   how does this happen
eroding orbits   crises
with no cure
your usual shine taking leave

Is this you   God
inching off   O God

do not
fall apart

Watch me   I might cry
or not

Before I Ask for Anything

> *. . . a confession*

Valiant were the days of you
jeeping through back fields

mud called *gumbo* flying helter-skelter
bottoming-out fully intended

We all wanted to be like you   wrecked & unflappable
skin merrily burned   tanned

then ashen   But   *Lord Almighty*   not like this
beaten to ruin   unable to rise   closing my eyes

as dusk dampens the senses and shame spreads
the harrowing grey   Its cloying grime

fouling the mind   Even here you are life
not death   scraping away

all my palsied secrets

I Talk into My Hands

> *... when you pray, go to your room, shut the door*

I talk into my hands as if they are
louvers   closed to all
but God   the invisible God
in whom the tang of dirty clothes and
darkness is no
              barrier
I sing into the darkness with animal pain
a kind of wailing like coyote's song
where holding the high note means
grateful something has died
              Anxiety
angles furtive glances through my fingers
as if being watched by an underdog   Yes
that kind of Savior   the quiet one
you wonder about
              Jesus
Almighty God   you   pinned down
too loud & ungodly   guttural sounds
call up dread   Closing your eyes forever
this the final effort   a tipping back of your head
and the howl

            I howl back

Fast and Shallow

Breathe   like a bird
stunned by a covert wall
What is glass to a songbird's keen eye
for hawks   Certainly this concussion is not a
raptor's drop & snatch   Nope   no way to describe
a slap down   so invisible   or the heart's persistent
& reckless beating on   or the way she lays
in stillness trying to forgive
what makes no sense
Finding nothing
just hurt

Claws

Invisible they trap me
         in bed
         rake my spine hip to rib
a clench
         without release
         I force my flesh
         to rise   I must
get up
         I have to   hold
         my breath
         beg   to breathe
Eternity & me
         on bed's edge   stock still
         mewling out a plea
         in the language of lifting
giving it all up

Glancing through
         the bars of blinds
         feathers of dawn glint   Heaven's
         barely gold eye
         my landscape   the spine of hills
         where prairie aligns with distant basins
         a straight horizon
         against rickety lines   those Vs of geese heave
a tremulous balance
     leaning upward
         lofting onto updraft
            as if flight is nothing
         nothing at all

but what will happen

Jesus   I say

                let it be like that
                      just   like   that   for me

Float Across Azure

August   hazy mid-afternoon   floating
across azure   an ascent
long wings silhouetted and soft

The smear of to & fro gives the slow gyre
a cadence of wandering
pleasure   Who can know

the mind of the hawk   how want & need
will this moment shiver

                a screeching halt
                mid-air

driven & dire   Hunger surges
Urgency & talons acquire

a new voice of prayer
body soul spirit   dropping
from heaven

Waiting for the Scan to Be Read
   or
Time between the Times

Between beginning and ends
the violet-blue eye of eternity stares
Within the endless dome   cirrostratus
ice crystalizes   and time stretches vacant but for

the finest falling snow   and shivers on bare skin
Gloom   infused with diamondous swirls
peppers every nerve   almost covering
a yaw   an oracle   Let's call it   the turn

by which night terrors fall and
heroes come to life   the two vaguely alike   disguised
in the warmth of wolf skins   No   from these
you cannot run   only close your eyes

wait for   something   some*one*
to decide to be caught with you
in the catastrophe   death
or a kiss   What will it be?

Enough for Today

Frozen shards lengthen
the way hunger heaves a sigh
patience marks time   and the imagination whittles specters

into the fog of waiting-for-results
Feral untamed idioms   the language of every scan

invade my fallow fields with a barely grey outline
Is that you Coyote

Stiff weeds test the air   Head down   relentless

he treads to the crest   as if that is the line
holding back the formidable   His terrors

are my terrors   loosed against tundra   My small lungs
and lips shrill a whistle   One pointed note

         gravely silences the whole valley
the way a wounded animal shrieks
like a wild dog turning   to stare at me

Should You Cover That

A dry shiv of bark   right there in the garden
See it   sprawled on the loam
next to that rounded tush   an innocent white
and barely pink bulb   the thin cover of skin
split   torn aside
dried   unaware

Should you cover that
he asked   and I thought the same

as I peered through the x-ray
the curve of my glutes an alluring line
barely visible and beautiful the way muscle
widens before it curls under
into plush vaginal
darkness   Everyone in the room pretends
to see nothing more
than my collapsing spine
the sacrum
and its hollow vertebrae   We stare
into the light
at what should be fixed   I mean
protected   hidden

Speaking of Weather

The call comes in
And you become   if not the diagnosis
then a cloud   a drippy mess without possibility

of ignoring tempest   typhoon   or the squall that doffs your cap
for you and covers hair with a faint tinkling of ice   Call it
weather or cancer   an act of God   It's a slashing flurry

casting a billion icy slivers   Chemo makes you so cold
where the port feeds past your heart   and you're deciding if life is
glacier or glisten   Lay your hand over that beating place

This valley is dark   horizontal   You watch atmospheric conditions
rise along the cold front   The thermal extends into the atmosphere
where haze rises and flaunts sharp outlines and shining edges

the words   *medicine* & *God*   defining a whole sky
      under cover of cumulous

Momma   Was It Like This

If it's too big to talk about
just say   Oh   *it's nothing*
And just like that   it'll be something

Yeah   Oh great   Now it's vaporous infinity
a fog with no beginning or end
and me sitting on a stump

the stupid place
where you take a deep breath
and start with   *One*   Something

so simple it's
almost cheating
That's what I do

Poverty

—she calls this the naked place

Shoved backward off a cliff   sheer
love of self quickens   flashes
Grabbing the air
        an alarming calm
        flops into freefall
        And a bottomless sigh
says this is giving up   Windless
weightless   I am   suspended without
grip or grit   here I am   almost gone
        and something
        still holding on

Holiest

The red-tail soars   seaming invisible
updrafts   amid the annoying hit & run
of a songbird   Why   I have no answers
I only watch as cancer
with intractable exploits   does a deadly job
I peck out a sound
like joy   too close to talons
and hooded eyes   pleading the protector
the strongest   holiest thing in the sky
to look at me   come after me
Help me

Burning with Ash

—nothing burns with ash unless it's been alive

Outside the warmth of these walls
open air expands   Smell the ozone   far-off rain
oxygen generously more available   No one knows why
sound changes after dark   as if the auditory range
of heaven covertly unfurls in the night

Warily the heart scours blackness for any scrap of light
whole constellations pause   mute   A sprinkler
splatters my direction   double-times it back
to the slow revving of frogs   and the distant
question of an owl   All this is about the way wind
and the Lord wait for us   out there   At wit's end

a rustle   then a star blinks   This is the way
I am invited into the secret built of brokenness   My own
flailing foments clouds of dust   until something like
wonder burns the sky vermillion   then darkens onto rock
ledges of soul   Oh   *glaze from heaven   repair*

heal me now   I go after God   striking my every word hard
against every fatal edge   And so we prove
each other   God's steely smack of flint
does not stop until a curl of my own heart ignites   drops
onto the char-cloth   and I plead   *please   dearest
tinder-nest of accrued prayer*

catch a stray spark

Come Back   Coyote

—symptoms spur the body to fight

    Coyote's hungry

and aloof
as undiscovered fractures
fault lines founder   My spine collapses again
mid-stride

    crossing the field

There I am going down in ragweed & thistle
Thus the helpless   quiesce   then
call out to God   who proceeds
to pronounce the name   Coyote
with all three syllables   The triune dog
turns and looks

    his golden tail

a sight that wells my soul   as if this is the miracle
to lift me
across the field

    Take me where I must go

The Boy Sweeping Whispered   Love Fiercely

Everyone's just trying to survive
this earth   Razor-sharp
talons empower raptors
a feet-first diving descent
and a grip that holds   like zip-ties

The captured rarely escapes

Watch the hawks overhead
aggressive swoops & dives
Wit & strength survive   forget about
obstacles or backing down   they soar
while maneuvering a massive wingspan
and nest only the highest ledges

Red-tails mate for life

feeding fledglings long after they've left the nest
The apex predator trains powerful
eyes on their slow ones   those lacking crucial
uplift potential
weak babies learning to fly
again
and again

from the ground up

Your Number's Up

—the terror of medical trials

        The clinic's a vast and teeming ant hill
a shimmering bucket of molten aluminum
with doctors gloved and methodical   A tech stands guard
over the heat   pours in the fiery medicament
The entrance bubbles & burns   Wait with me while this cools
        Brutally
exposed   this last chance incinerates every hallway & lesion
Blood vessels boil every fast-growing cell   Baby cancers
have no chance   Death curls inside and out   with
or without answers
        Apocalyptic revelation
it's called digging up remains   All that molten metal   Every bit
of air congealed   tumorous   Evidence is unearthed   scrubbed
Each passageway of the soul's grotto   tactile now   Hell the very
air of an entire colony scrubbed to a sheen
        Yet thousands
scurry toward the hopeful place   experimental love scribbled
on prescriptions   Hope tripping over thresholds of egress & death
heartbeats vanish in failure   dead ends   Lives powder into urns
shaped for all the world like a place to grow
        Do not think you can
relegate this scourge   all I have left   to variables less than zero
and a few unknowns   as if the places my life has traveled
will not retain a body   of knowledge and awe   empty places
refusing to mirror back horror

Wings and Hollow Bones

Long Nights' Moon

—God and apex predators

There in the darkest month   a scintilla called full
but furtive   a glow barely reflects from the farthest reach

while nightmare's bark and bay echoes
night & day   *Get down Give up*
         Give in   stay inside

Dusk continues   O God   who spins
winter moons   each slim revolution
begets uncertain smiles and   can I say
threats   Jackal of the Mind circles
he's circling the days   repeating a low
growl that means   attack

I'm given the smallest shot   a pinprick of light
racing straight toward me   No not a train
more like someone calling my name
in the boreal night   A Presence behind
penumbra

the thinnest halo

On The Observation Deck: A Resuscitation

—a continuous one-way stream of air

Bird lungs extend
into the bone   So no   bird bones
are not merely hollow   they're pneumatized

Think of oxygen as need   immense as prayer
or dreams where you are under water
retching & choking   and only recover when
forced to breathe
in & out
at the same time   Chemo   certain death
to all fast-growing cells   followed by rescue
with my own stem cells   Circular breathing
This is what it takes
to fly

Canada Geese Sail

Wild geese sweep across the haze
and horizon of mid-winter   slow sketchy
movement   the way a body moves
with cancer   All the muscles of the back
converge   collude to protect a fragile spine
as easily as each bird aligns
       no jerky spasms
           just a rhythmic handing off
               of fatigue that comes
         from leading others
     without question
concern   or thought
as if we all knew this was coming
and had rehearsed the navigation   traversed
the whole blue sky   with an eye for packs
of coyotes below   making overpowering this killer
look simpler   than all
the honking might imply

When My Head Is Cold

Wispy threads of charity
drape over the bald places   It's a kind of scrawl
thoughts from good hearts   longhand warmth
to remind me who I am   rub my cheek
And yet it does not help me to say
the hardest words

        It's the losses that hope to save me

I'm thinking of David leaning his head   looking afar
as if God were the prodigal   Way off over there
his own guilt runs after God's own heart   down the hillside
dodging rubble & rock   depression & dent
almost as if the bluff itself wants to rise
to meet his feet   and lift the world
closer to what faith cannot say
or properly explain   when the next step
feels nothing at all like the way home

When I Pray to Be Healed

A dimming kind of strength
swings low and to the south
Dependable sun favors
the horizon   Late afternoon flares

It's November again   Life stuck in a window
the rosemary plant blooms for a whole summer
a continuous mystery
Look   small blue flowers
still coming on

Perhaps these wingéd luminaries
holding to topmost branches
are my protectors

silent   euphoric
like a raptor's motionless
soar   chased by a worry of finches

All Ears

        Only ears
waggle above the horizon   Two coyotes
consult as I round the hillside
Bumping shoulders slightly
      they toss
no more than a glance my way   It's early February
misty fog   but I saw it   that look
     Race you to the bottom
Feral wildness it's a risky invitation   Here I am
holding tight to my string of days   every morning's groan
a call to prayer   God   why do I think you might
      tame
disease or wild dogs
erase their violence that cannot save
or obliterate instinctive & savage strength
that preys on the fragile
      Coyote
I admit I prayed your brutal beauty might bless me
one more time   before I go   And look there you are
not one but two miracles   glancing off each other
      racing
down the other side to the next hill
as if I might   I should somehow
give chase

Instruction in Case You Wake Early

—fig: the sweetest fruit of all

I stand   but hang   onto the bedpost   pull
a ragged cord   lift the dusty blind   We kiss
in a predictable honey-grey flush
You   my love   are horizon   stubborn
rooted as the place called home   with that beast
of a fig tree out back   claimed as our own

at least for this season   Come   Beloved
crawl with me   inside this not-so-pretty fruit
where flowers bud   safely bloom   hidden
within the heart of the fig   Those tiny wasps
most unlikely pollinators in the world
give up antennae and wings   just to get in
and crawl between you & me & the drupes
Then die   Thus within the grim life of sacrifice

you and I have become
the bleak ways of love   still and always
leading to the sweetest fruit

Sigh too Brief to Mention

A leafy tremble flickers across the thicket
Any reason at all to gaze beyond you
and the enduring exhale we call serious
conversation

Whoosh   out of the tree emotion airborne   Just like that
a billion little fears take off   take over
The mind unleashes an entire flock of blackish birds as
anger charges aloft   one fluid mass   iridescent
insistent on being heard   The whole sky's a-swirl
to & fro   alive with small begging sounds   peeps & whines
a snapping of the bill leading to longer elaborate melodies
Squawk & screech   words fly   we vie   intensify
arc & turn   A momentary lead

vanishes in updrafts & churlish drops

Leaf or bird   word for word   This is about wind
How it doesn't quit   it just eventually dies
taking with it gusts
that fill our breath with loss

Our hearts
land just shy of the thicket
Something barely beating
remembers itself

No one says look   but there they are
your eyes
reflective mosaics of nethermost blues

And me inside them   staring back
into the promise to love

with a sigh too brief to mention

The Burden of Gifts

For you I choose train whistles
the far-off moans
waking me with warnings
hurtling toward me   invisible
bumpbumps of iron
wheels   like our two wills
unable to stop
and   O Lord   you know
this is about the crossings

I've never crossed myself like a Catholic
I doubt
such small gestures affect much
but under the covers I go ahead
and cross the expanse
of bed to touch you with a toe
A kind of signal for you
after you've fallen asleep
that I've slowed   to let the danger pass

The Wonder of Weeping

—Orison (a prayer of supplication)

On the other side of the glass
a finch alights   The woman holds her breath
to see if this too will flitter on   or cock its head
fearless   Deer browse

through the remains
of yesterday's galling storm
branches denuded   snapped
brokenness blown asunder

and these innocents brave the aftermath
nosing out
sweet round apples
fallen from high places

Marriage
or
Earth's Own Smell

> *... the fragrance emitted by a thousand flowers*
> *absorbs into the pores of rocks or soil*

Our life together has been spent
finding rocks   Off colors of granite & agates
pile in the studio   where you and I wire
unlikely and awkward rubble
with bits of wood and song   the neck
of my violin   his chin rest   that old cedar shingle
turned fret board   remnants of longevity   Key changes
modulate up & down   Sticks & stones
hummm a cadence
an almost recognizable
melody   I sing out
Do we like this stone
Nope   he says   *love is something*
more like rain

Very funny
no rocks won't drip & flow   torrent or trickle   Thunder
cannot be wired in   Without earthy findings we've nothing
to hang onto   Lightning
the strident flash we both wait for
slashes at our darkness

This is where he takes all the rocks outside
digs a hole and lays them to rest

He shucks into bags a mountain of driftwood
collected pegs   a fingerboard   scrolls

In low tones we watch each other's nakedness

Every now and then
he wanders outside   comes in
palming a dirty rock   He drags me to the kitchen
We drench it under the faucet
then stand by the sink   the smell of rain
between us

Seventeen Houseplants

I apologize to you for not knowing
        all your names
or caring too much about water   I am sorry
        primrose and impatiens
I do admire your faces   and you perennials rebounding
        like relatives   who've made it
thus far   staying surprisingly green
        and still growing   but always
turning   returning toward more
        sun
All those roots settle down in the dark
        with rayless and secret channels of longing
These little anchors embody
        ever-present thirst   wizened champions
drawing water out of hardpan
        Marvelous little lives buried down there survive
cimmerian shade
        and don't try too hard to figure it out

        I'm like you
Gone for a while   Always coming back
        helps

Honey from a Rock

This is about the way people hold words
a lush bouquet in sweaty fingers
about how hard it was   is

It is hard   to feel what someone else feels   like gratitude
a giant sequoia in the prickly bewilderment
of cancer   stumbling over shallow

roots & stems   That friend gathering pluck   staring
into my eyes   smiling so big I thought perhaps he'd shout
his son   TAH DAH   is no longer disabled

but no his hand finds my arm   like *bless you* after a sneeze
or a pat on the back of the persistent
obligation to be happy for goodness

yet unseen   Gathering his dreads into a band he calls
the believer's advantage   my friend jabbers out
what I've been thinking   *Why me*

He's mystified   and without explanation

for the monsoon   The flood of everything
every single thing   he ever hoped he'd get   he has
Right now   *I got it*   *Here it is*   *Just look* he says

with a full swing of arms past his son toward and across
around the vast circle where earth meets sky

Heaven touches earth

Mud until Today

. . . the dream of waking

The mulish footslog of interminable overcast   A yearlong
forecast of risk   skulks the sog
she called her garden   Too much mud but   it's warmer today

    She loosens the polka dot scarf around her neck

All elbows   ants by the thousands eat away the nectar
enclosing tender buds   The garden greening up   almost ready
for a comeback   O Lord   over there

    more ants

managing soft bodied aphids   milking out waste   The sticky
honeydew
lives on   Destruction mates & propagates   She swallows thickly
thinking   *Can this be good*   Her spine now fixed

    but smaller   The scarf wrinkled and curling   drops to the ground

unanswered questions emerge   insignificant   irrelevant
beside a boisterous explosion of roses   And a scandalous
splurge of peonies   Spine tingling summer

Exaudi Nos   Domini (Hear us   Lord)

I've unlocked the back door again
slipped out & into
        the mighty black cloak
        of Polaris
Here you are ever-guiding giant
watching over everything that dares
be done in the dark   the earthy din of those
fallen stars called men   Orion   great hunter
please stand down   What I mean is even you
must thirst   Go ahead take a draught from
the Big Dipper   great ladle on high
whose end points
        durably North
      as if a compass
           is exactly what is needed
                a witness to every trip and misdeed
                a benevolent guide that allows for a little
frog noise   a distant bird   Is that you Coyote
listening to wind in trees   An aspen quavers
as if what is needed is not a score   but a nod

A Song in This Place

Blood Moon

> *. . . tumor less now,*
> *head wrapped like a war hero*

Her beloved takes her hands   says
Give me your troubles
and thus the language of being one
resumes exhaustive care of each other

She would do this for him   and them   those

who prayed for a stranger
who took her where she never wanted to go
always asking the same thing

Given the choice   would she embrace it all again

the tumor   an abscess
a piece of fake skull   the pulse of cancer

She guesses so

for who can know goodness for sure

without sidling up
to horror's dark side   And there

finding oneself
glad to be alive

Momma　　What Did You Call

that hangnail not trimmed　　but pulled on　　ripped back
with a drop of blood　　the burning secreted
to your mouth　　without interjection　　Was there a word for

worse when your brother died　　Was it words or his bottle
shushing what was favorite between you　　I watched you
hold back love　　a reluctance to see life frozen in death

What about when they opened you and saw
the horror of a billion cancers　　is there a word for locating
the ileostomy right where you need to bend　　Is it

called the terror of insides coming out unexpectedly and
your own putridity　　a shit bag　　imminent danger of dislodge
defining you　　Meaning nothing you can do

on your own　　Remember when Daddy
said helping you was his privilege　　the hammer of humility
causing you a thousand deaths　　What is that word

the reflection of love　　or pity　　in your beloved's eyes
So much less now remained of you
it must have seemed like a small thing　　to ask

your physician husband to inject a vial of mercy
　　　　Suffering
him saying he cannot

The Conductor's Baton

> *... the greatest strain in life is waiting for God*

Birdsong
vanishes   An arresting rhapsody
reels & retreats   The concerto rehearsal
collapses
into quiescence
No one moves   everyone knows this score's
performance
requires
straining in the dark   quashing   unfledged outbursts

holding that first note with utmost clarity
but waiting   dumbly
to begin
the chorus recited   learned   relearned
echoed   Listen this is
not strictly melodious   but a pitch of hope
becoming
frightfully noisy

Until the oboe's *A*   shifts the brood
toward necessity   Utter silence

of voice
and wing
faith fixed

on the scepter's
rise

Summon This Kind of Prayer

—syrinx: a two-sided voice box

Little wood thrush
Tip your head back   trill or whistle   Overtones
rarified & clear   stun the air
like angels standing behind you

    How does one learn this breaking
    of the voice in two
    this swallowing down all that is
    singular   even   as the thought of dissonance

        cries against the bone of the chest
        Din rushes the skull where   desperation
        whimpers against   dire need
        for air
        barely able to get out a
        prayer   where

            head
            and heart
            sing both parts

                without thinking

An Incident

> ... *"fight" and "battle" often appear*
> *within four words of "cancer"*

I've outlasted the bad   old Hans says
standing mid-street
no longer waiting for something
better   He scoots the walker
and turns   a perfect half circle
without words   Hans stares straight
past fated circles and bags of 87 years
red rimmed eyes of light blue
blue like the hottest stars
still alive

I said   *Be careful   jumping that curb*
and something broke
across his face   a smile
with dimples on both sides   It was
the wink of a soldier letting go
of fear
with a crisp nod   As if in charge
for a moment   I had sent
him back to battle   to fight
for what can never be retrieved

When a Rib Tears Away

A small pop just above the sternum
and what used to be a hug   becomes a twinge
the dreaded ebb & flow   pain & recoil
Tell me how a small fissure   a meager rift
can torture life from one side of my world
to the other   all night   an endless sleepless
rant   Why oh why does the ache rise

at 4 am   As if it was
no more than a robin tipping his head
side to side   golden beak   brightly
announcing the light of another day

I'm watching that bird go on and on
mending secret feathers
     no one sees

          mangled splays   her beak
          splicing the frayed

            hooking the tiniest barbs
            smoothing   soothing

        my soul   despite
        the hurt   Giving the torn

    soul strength
    sheen

A remedy
of small darns

Wind Crying to Get In

A massive runoff roared   Eroded mud
surged   smashed boulder & streambed
Amid urgent snow & unfinished conversations
I'd hung on like aspen leaves
in February   brittle & dry
not yet willing to let go of life   All that quaking

through the deadly winter   cataclysm here then gone
like I'm safely down the pike   but for that ghostly
plastic bag billowing up off the freeway   Its haunted
rising off the middle of the street   hovers midair
chasing the surviving part of me
off the thoroughfare   bashing into the median
where old wounds emerge

with ropey scars
Wind persists
rattles the door of my mind
Sky cries with cold   to come in
and trouble my fire

Putting on a Swimsuit

Diminished spinal length means   a pooched-out belly
There it is along with slumpy shoulders   the curled-slouch
and forward-lean of a hunchback   I force
my shoulders down to make deformity acceptable

Salvation called cemented vertebrae   refuses any new arch
or twist   The usual grace of swinging myself down
onto the pool edge in one fluid motion   stutters
a mechanical question   splays me onto the deck   Over-

stretching the guarded spine   I bungle off the edge
into depths of breath-halting cold   Face-me-down
in the water   Toes find the wall and remember

to push off   flashbacks of learning to swim
As feet sink   fear shoves
my face   further   deeper in

Surely I will be given a new center of gravity
Water itself will forgive my horror
hold me aloft   hide me in arms

where faith floats amid the remnants   destruction
& reconstruction find the fast-water   the perfect blend
of water-surface & air   Buoyancy and near drowning

She Says You Get What You Get

It's windy on the porch
She props a gimpy leg on a wooden chair
exposes it to sun   She says you get what you get

Ever mumbling to God for attention   something like
look at me look at me and *oh wow* there it is
another bruise blooming just below the knee

She turns her face to the sky   and draws
a patient breath   In prayer-like motion
she smears salve over the parch of skin
a pauper's salvation

where pity for a sick thing takes on something akin to
gladness for some attention   Despite the defect
now it's hard to hate
what she loves   The broken parts
she hands back to God

Sugar Moon
   or
There is No Cure   Yet

I touch the still numb
scar on my head   something twinges
under scarce new hair and shivers down my neck   I'm thinking
of maple trees   waiting   and waiting

through another phase of the moon
how one must wait for the whole earth
to lean   before warming arrives   Icy nights roll over
Sun breathes away from earth   Temperature

dips   Flaws and fissures
line the maple's bark
But wood next to the heart
has awakened   A sweet tonic rises   That's all it takes

The holiness of a little sap
          explodes   bark ruptures
                misplaced hope shatters
          in the late freeze
concusses like gunshot

The Uncertainty Principle

I watch the muscle of his jaw
clench

The no-show
of faith ticks him off

about now being considered
lost   Well   more like left out

and he's kind of mad about
someone thinking he can be missing

what he doesn't know
can't see or feel

Something inside pecks at
the notion of invisible care

the way a stupid sparrow
mindlessly rides an updraft

Pure nothing   But I can tell
he's in   See   it's called flying

Emptiness moves aside for him
ground still firm and forever there

as endless wonder   beats its wings
against ever arriving

Too Close to My Eyes

Too close to my eyes   the black and blue
dragonfly stalls

stares into me   and zips to the arborvitae
I imagine its shrug

floating down between us
a tingle where the instant remains

gilded inside me   And then for you Beloved
I'll sigh and try again to explain that miracle

My fingers will mime & gesture
recite & confess the bright moment as if

the love God whispered to me
could mean anything at all

to you

Memorial

—outside the clinic

Smoke & wax   Glassed-in
candles flicker against chain-link   On the sidewalk
roses & rocks
line up to resemble a heart   the bric-a-brac

of impotence   Something that is now nothing
Another mother shoves a child's shoulder
and tells her to *drop it*
Leave it

the stuffed animal   Something dearly loved
dies
and loss spits in the face
of everyone standing there

who thought their prayers
meant peace

The Day Before We Leave Seattle

—with a nod to M. Champlin

He said *You smile too much*
meaning I think you read poems without
any concept of timing   thunder arriving before flash
the rain the rain the rain   oversoaking
all reliable places to stand
        under the eaves
where everyone's counting seconds
till this is over   Yes we got it   Those miles
of curbs & gutters empty the rush
onto the street   A spreading fan of the cataract
mirrors jagged lightening
        Still we don't flinch at the unexpected
house fire   We know exactly how to feel
about the dog caught inside
the way things loved must be saved
in the end   and still we stay straight-faced
while sirens & smoke & clouds
stare each other down   Hold us that way
        through the turn
Restrain yourself against the naïve
grin   the smile
that makes us wonder
if a storm ever happened

Exposure

—the naked seed

You know the secret meaning of dead-end
sitting by yourself   squinting
through the fly-specked window
greyed with sediment from watering   That crack
across the lower left   No way to fix it
close the wound   or step through it into the night

Remember the moon   surrounded by trifles of light   Those
starry giants hanging above   intensify what it means
to be   alone   but not alone   in a promised land
that still holds all the myths and dreams
you must live   Yes they ring in your ears

lowing for what used to be your life   Dusk to dawn
who can lay there   give it all up the way Isaac
survived the smoke and stillness between molecules
walking back home   Stripped that bare

My New Name

—means vanishing point

Cancer makes me sound stupid   speaking present tense only
No stepping back to past   no future

I've become a gerund   an *ing* on every verb   succumbing
to the immutable right-now ever-beating heart-pace
the open-ended essence of ongoing life   Listen to me now
still humming another verse   composing a chorus cantillating
risks & tumors & healings

Every glance forward or back is reduced to nacre   iridescence
not clarity   Being alive is a gate made of pearl
each moment hinged on one post   like a name
that opens all the doors   Call me Everlasting

A Valley Wide as Spring

Mowers   dogs   dandelions & cut grass
and oh look   those flying fluff balls
bright yellow finches   ubiquitous bird-noise
a kind of approval dashes round about
till late in the day   when my faint & famished tribe
traipses in
                A hush comes over every sunburned
heart   crowded into the living room   My body's
awkward endurance has no offering
for the day   no accomplishment   no
raison d'être   Not-dead-yet grips
everyone's thoughts   They are tied
elbow-to-elbow   hip-to-hip   in a perfect guilt-cramp
           where everyone chokes on not asking
How are you
Fine already clots the air   Stare
at your shoes   clear phlegm from your throat
And as if wonder is all that is needed
a little stick drops off a sleeve to the floor
            something to look at
freeing the room from thick and humid
pity   And yearning to get back to
something called normal
            You never know
I may just chirp through another year
and there I'll be
living proof   next spring
Think of it   me
nesting again

Escape

... and then this breaks out swift as a swallow

Resignation
sneaks in during the tightest turns   rubber-necking
as life biffs into the next protocol

complete with rebound anxiety   Cancer's a raptor
heading for mud-daubed twigs & leaves &
trash   I'm watching the way a swallow then gives in

to instincts   its blue-green innate
otherness knows more than it knows as unseen enemies
assail with shrieking alarm and curious ticking
as if time itself must scare everyone   Where goes courage

Dropping flopping   unfinished fatigue trips on the ground
faintly wounded and easy pickings   Gawkers
perch in trees   on lines   Surging bird noise heightens
a fountainhead   a go-for-broke   swarming

spree   A remedy of ruckus   the murmuration breaks free
on no more than the lightest breeze   An uprising where
every stray thought finds horizon   wing-to-wing   Prayers
at home in thin air

A Hawk Does Not Have a Song

Hawk is the Song

Sunrise and Moonset

The Lord behind and before

Out in the wastelands
enduring a whole year of camping
part of the wilds   she's brrr-cold despite the best
down bag   Every morn squirming into jeans
sweatshirt & socks   hating to leave
that tent   the warm sack   breakfast sizzling

over tinder and sparks   That is until one day
a new dawn shrugs
says *Time to go*
And no   no fire this morning

No more fire
She's told   *Stand in the light*
So that's what she does   Stands   Faces the sun

Her beloved turns the other way
Keeping an eye on dubious shadows
he readies for the unknown   facing
the depth of darkness   edging his whole being
into the uncharted
hoping to God   he has her back
Hoping like hell   God has his

Immortal Invisible

                Throw open the windows   belt out
endless anthems of salvation Upward heave praise brassy barefaced noise
before dawn   come hell or the hawk   Awaken the wee-small & drabbest
      among us   those who cower   alone & tongue-tied   Oh dread
        no more   Scan not the horizon   Stand up straight   Choir
              a voice of the centuries   Summon the sky to

                      resounding remembrance
                            Evidence of
                                  God

Coyote Alive

I saw coyote again   loping
through the brume   as if
unwavering wind was on his side   That is
until he saw the walkers of dawn
and had to choose

between man afoot
and the narrow path between houses
One day I suppose someone
will trap or shoot him   all bravado
and pride   Who in the world
wants wild hope   stuffed & dusty
hunkered down in the den   But there I am

at the window every morning
scanning dawn
for untamed movement   a nod of wind
feral fear giving hope
another chance to be lithe

Transfiguration

I wonder if he arrives early
and sees the children
scatter and scour the bookshelves and floor
Under beds   behind the piano   the littles
whisper to each other   *Where is it?*
Where IS it?   The book   That one   you know the one
One sofa   two cushions   too crowded
for everyone to have a good seat   I wonder
if he is surprised how long his stories hold the children
gazing straight ahead   Imagine
coaxing them into a furious climb   joining
the unflinching scale   casting off rope & axe
As a last resort   suspending all disbelief
Somewhere near the top

ahead of them   he stops

their mouths open
As if this is the final switchback
every child turns from the pages to look at his face
watch

and there it is   How long did it take
to hear again his baritone
from the edge of the world

Do not be afraid

Thirst of Shore Meets Parch of Water

A coupling   sand & water   Awash with clashing
the suck of tide pulls the whole ocean sideways
Ripples & waves spit out froth   As if by force
the moon chooses a side   lines up regiments   Breakers surge

a constant running up the shore then grinding back down
Rip tides echo the same old brawl   Brine billows
overtakes the silence of shore   ramming against her perpetual
lack of response   The insistent curl rises again

pauses in swelled turbulence   and falls all over itself
The gravity of attraction remains powerful   beautiful
Imperium roars   floods over corral & shell   boulders & agate
urging the whole strand to let loose its treasures   yet

the beach   the very ground   stonewalls
disinclined to concede higher ground
The ancient boundary holds
for now

Behind the Blinds

I dread rising   again   having been awake
for hours   waiting
to hear you come down the hall
I imagine the sound of molecules   tiny   fading
stars of night dropping from your heels
on the hardwood
falling faster and louder as you come in
and lift the shades   and fling wide
the outside door   the one I never open
without a good reason
as if today is the day
I must face surrender   How heaven rushes in
      cold as winter rain
the fierce gale   a blurring fury
      And I am
      frozen
in a shock of pure white light
      That's me
on the edge of healing   a shiver
opening myself to being saved

17 Degrees   Snow   Blinding Light

Beloved   you and I live
like two sorrels
standing as still as the pause
between breaths   our marriage almost filling
this early morning circle of sunlight

enclosing us and the barbed wire fence
Longer hairs on winter muzzles
are frosted   Look   almost touching
their haunches quiver

Large dark eyes gaze sunward
unmoved by malignancies   A thin fog
veils our heads   I am warmed
and brightened by the mystery

how expired sighs hover with brilliance at dawn
as one's own breath continues to drift
away   evanescent over a ridge
spreading across the whole valley

Though the world remains vaguely blue
with cold   and all the landmarks persist in place
light holds with tenderness   those
still breathing

Red-Tailed Hawk

Two red-tails sail the azure   spirals dip & script
soaring grab & runs   they grapple & spin   talons intertwine
lock   As one
they plummet out of sight
              O Lord
the effortless loss   and astonishing upward arc of just one
ending so near my window   I gasp

        Time holds

        Hovers
                hovering

Too long it's been too long
O Lord   for flight

        to pause

           full stop

                chest braced outward
                and frozen

there it is
a cross of muscle and plumage facing the sun
brilliance infusing
something akin to gold
            in a hawk's eye   This isn't passion
or mating
but severe excellence

life   neither aware
nor unaware of God
            the two
               perfectly one

Symptoms of Morning

Flinging hollow bones
over vetch & thistle   killdeer
dart & chase   race
the smell of spring   lilac & rose
Chimeric impatience
flutes past a pile of slash
branches of hope   finding their way
back to dirt   These are winter prayers
collapsed
under a copse of pine
Memorized verses
you never thought would help

Time Disappears (while painting)

Hours minutes seconds cannot be
wiped on   or up   Like titanium white

a lifetime passes colorless   until brightened
by complements

the way orange smudged into ultramarine
converts to grey   *Ohhh*   you say

thinking   that is a good color
for clouds   exactly

the moment before sun breaks through
although you know this flash might be   nothing

a glimpse of the divine   scuffing scumbles of gold & vermillion
into a simple thin line   separating

earth & sky   the way a reflection flips
what is up what is down   A shazam   Illusion

holds you suspended in relief
you had no idea you needed

the way I might heave a sigh
and then remember   one more time

evermore   I am alive

He of Old Age Died

. . . to those without hope   hope is given

Life stops
No muscular breathing   bellowing air in & out
No screen-like gills to slip oxygen between worlds
Nearby roses no longer replenish the air

He called Inge
his *Rosa Floribunda*   cold-hardy and secretly fragrant
Just once Hans left her   for Seattle succor   They waited
years to be Americans   call it war penance   Funny what holds

a marriage together
But skip to the end   where Inge dies   Hans stands it
toddering & shrunken   He cloisters himself in the back yard
among the finches   watches them in an ambush of downpour

disappear
Grief insists on being a failure of heart   every organ
refusing nourishment   Swollen ankles flood over his shoes
Starvation of heart bloats his belly

and lungs until nothing
beats effectively   Hans hides inside
his head   unaware how the magnificent heart compensates
overcompensates   then drowns itself

Live
no more it insists   I walk past Hans's house
It's November   yet abloom
with the breath of rosa floribunda

Dear Hawk

Was that you on my walk
watching from the trees   an undoing that's been evolving
for days now   I quit staring at the cat's car-crushed
body   after that one eye

ceded the fixed gaze   as if finally yes   *yes*
the Wild Blue Yonder might after all take a soul
this far into rigor mortis   I'm wondering about Lazarus
wandering back to a brand-new old life

like a tabby cat   one eye and one paw
looking just fine   an old & new life   but no words   A throat
but no explanations   Even you   Red-tail   that rasping
screee   hushed now   Have you flown to the brink

in your life without words   Might I mistake you   for a hunter
a cat
a songbird

Lunula

> *—half-moon at the base of the nail*

I have my mother's thumb
spare flesh binding a stout knuckle   the nail
square   with a distinct ridge

running the left side   Half-moon o' self
you wax and wane like she did   managing
need   delirium   the lusty cry of earth's lullaby

Yes   we suffer   life long and hard to finish
She in me neatly embedded
lifelong   like a hymn that holds on

Finding You Again

A Husband Poem

My beloved slept downstairs
last night   Eventide to dawn
gray and mute   and colder
Restless waking lifts my head hourly
all night long   straining
to hear any draft   a current
the slightest   murmurish   sigh
that means   you live
you're alive
rolling toward me again
breathing in my face   cleaving
to my side   even in sleep

Prayer Without Words

Just under the bark
she sees a beetle has gnawed dinner
into a tracery   Tunnels & caves
line the lumbering giant
a script encrypted
on sapwood

Out of the ocean not long ago
she dragged this chunk of oak
gently laid the waterlogged timber
atop the hearth   and dried the marvelous drift
Five hundred years circle and hieroglyphs
hold vigil   An oracle on an ingle of stone
A primordial prophet
passes a message forward

She keens with longing for the ancient
prayers and the urge to sing
in the eternal language of light   Soon
the pith smokes and sparks
roars into flame
as if this was never about song or words
but offering up
all that would warm her

Plumage   The Wing and Its Mighty Elbow

Maybe my soul is paper after all   so easily torn
smoothing wrinkles of reason into faith

putting two and two back together   telling
the vaulted heavens not to lay those blues on my water

Cancer cannot pronounce deliverance   Ever I am dumb
to its dim voice   a blind crone

feeling across the table
for bread   instead of a candle   an offering of dry crumbs

for the bird who cannot fly   cannot stay aloft   but for wind
and ever unseen forces rushing   shifting against her

Tonight the whispering has gone quiet   A little leaf noise
in the trees would be fine

Your shirt made my prayer closet smell like wind
That's all I know for now

Selah   To Understand More Than a Sentence

There is no clearing away the tickle
the dryness   gruffing away the constriction
in the throat   How long
did Moses perch   transfixed   on his knees
facing mortiferous holiness
before risking a careful breath   tacitly
holding it   through the slow shaky rise
head down   always down   only
touching a bare toe
to a square of light that slipped in
under the great curtain

The Precipice

Incandescence   strikes the rimrocks
the sonorous display fades

like cymbals   and the aftermath of glory
jing-jangles my dozing   as if God himself

now covers the sun   Mute clouds
cram the heavens   churn fists of wind

To the bleak blasts   I turn my back
Hazy splendor

vanishes as if pleasures of life thus far
cannot be eternal   The thought of never being healed

immobilizes every drop
of the will   One viable spinal nerve shivers

in belief
There could be more

Care Giver

Thin fingers
entwine around walking sticks

you and I
linger over the pale coin of a moon at noon

eclipsed by wings
three red-tailed hawks   circling

eyeing my shaven head
the slit & scar tracking

a question mark   mid-brow to ear
The brain   my mind   cowering

under the missing chunk of skull   pulsing
and miraculous   horrible   I guess

One thin scalpel incised
script against bone

picking up speed the way a skater
holds an edge

against the smallest pause
and so gains momentum

before toe plant
the leap and spin

and lift   Oh the lift
of you and me

walking home together

What Happened

    —the anniversary

New moons reappear   every month for years
Memories sharp as that first silvery curl of light
        waxing out of blackness   another flare
the unthinkable brain tumor flawlessly expunged   a month later
the cleft breeds infection   Full moon   here it comes
        the anniversary with splintery edges   a larger circle
of skull taken and not replaced right away
as if skin alone affords sufficient cover
over sanguineous operations   There's no escape
        from retracing steps   every careful footfall
it takes to get face-to-face with this now
terrible God   and how I climbed onto the bench
        next to him   edging onto his lap   leaning
into the chest of Almighty   and the pulse
of that heartbeat   the twining
meander of a single note
        an unchangeable key
            a hail to me alone
                a presence
that cannot be folded
or managed   more like a smell   a seasoning
seeping into and through
my being   Every year
                      there it is
carried on my back   like wings   Constantly
I look over my shoulder
hoping to glimpse   what
has happened
to me

An Afterword

Breath Holding

After two years there is no noise
        outside
        and within me   Has something left?
        Is anything left
        to hold?   I am alive
as the rope called safety slips away   the end
        not tied?   Tests disperse like dust
        Points no longer stick to reports
        graphs pile like kindling
        What is done and cannot be changed   covers
my ears   A whisper of tomorrow
        whirls like the spinning of seasons   Setting out
        taking off
        feels migratory   like a shove
        OK I'm leaving   all set   for what?   where?
Am I only a sky-bird   risking
        raptor talons?   Have I yet a place in the great
        murmuration? O let it be
        with my beloved   There it is again
        that slight bend   a shift   without spasm
The lifting of fear

Soli Deo Gloria

Acknowledgments

There would be no sound to the words in this book without my beloved husband Dana.

There would be no echo into eternity without my family.

Words defy the gratitude and affection I feel toward those who have traveled these past years with me. My dearest Traveling Companions, I love you more than you know.

Bethany Schafer, thank you for conversation, your thoughts, especially in "What Happened."

Laurie Klein, reader extraordinaire, if that was it, your help would be and has been exceptional. I have been privileged to call you friend. You understand, uncover blind spots, and heal. The poetry and prayer we share—a gift.

Kathy M., Teresa B., and Janet G. you are true friends: heart, backbone, muscle in my life.

D.S. Martin, editor and poet, thank you for consummate attention to both detail and heart in my work. Your perspective and broad insight are exceptional.

I am grateful to the editors of the following journals and anthologies in which these poems first appeared (sometimes in a different form):

Cultivating Project: "Holiest"
    "On the Observation Deck: A Resuscitation"
    "Selah: to Understand More Than a Sentence"

Acknowledgments

Ekstasis: "What Happened"

Fathom: "Seventeen Houseplants"
  "Memorial"
  "Fast and Shallow"

KPBS Spokane Public Radio, The Poetry Moment: "To Save a Robin"

McMaster Journal of Theology & Ministry: "Coyote Alive"
  "Sunrise and Moonset"
  "Transfiguration"

Mockingbird: "Finding You Again"

Presence: "Exaudi Nos, Domini"

Radix: "The Bride of Christ Considers the Upcoming Wedding"
  "The Wonder of Weeping"
  "Agree to Disagree"
  "Prayer Without Words"

Tale of Two Trees: "Robin"
  "I Talk into my Hands"
  "Waiting for the Scan to be Read"
  "Come Back Coyote"

Tweetspeak: "Lunula"

The Poiema Poetry Series

COLLECTIONS IN THIS SERIES INCLUDE:

Six Sundays Toward a Seventh by Sydney Lea
Epitaphs for the Journey by Paul Mariani
Within This Tree of Bones by Robert Siegel
Particular Scandals by Julie L. Moore
Gold by Barbara Crooker
A Word In My Mouth by Robert Cording
Say This Prayer into the Past by Paul Willis
Scape by Luci Shaw
Conspiracy of Light by D.S. Martin
Second Sky by Tania Runyan
Remembering Jesus by John Leax
What Cannot Be Fixed by Jill Pelaez Baumgaertner
Still Working It Out by Brad Davis
The Hatching of the Heart by Margo Swiss
Collage of Seoul by Jae Newman
Twisted Shapes of Light by William Jolliff
These Intricacies by David Harrity
Where the Sky Opens by Laurie Klein
True, False, None of the Above by Marjorie Maddox
The Turning Aside anthology edited by D.S. Martin
Falter by Marjorie Stelmach
Phases by Mischa Willett
Second Bloom by Anya Krugovoy Silver
Adam, Eve, & the Riders of the Apocalypse anthology edited by D.S. Martin
Your Twenty-First Century Prayer Life by Nathaniel Lee Hansen
Habitation of Wonder by Abigail Carroll
Ampersand by D.S. Martin
Full Worm Moon by Julie L. Moore
Ash & Embers by James A. Zoller

Acknowledgments

The Book of Kells by Barbara Crooker
Reaching Forever by Philip C. Kolin
The Book of Bearings by Diane Glancy
In a Strange Land anthology edited by D.S. Martin
What I Have I Offer With Two Hands by Jacob Stratman
Slender Warble by Susan Cowger
Madonna, Complex by Jen Stewart Fueston
No Reason by Jack Stewart
Abundance by Andrew Lansdown
Angelicus by D.S. Martin
Trespassing on the Mount of Olives by Brad Davis
The Angel of Absolute Zero by Marjorie Stelmach
Duress by Karen An-hwei Lee
Wolf Intervals by Graham Hillard
To Heaven's Rim anthology edited by Burl Horniachek
Cup My Days Like Water by Abigail Carroll
Soon Done with the Crosses by Claude Wilkinson

www.ingramcontent.com/pod-product-compliance
Lightning Source LLC
Chambersburg PA
CBHW051657040426
42446CB00009B/1187